HAPPINESS

An Essay

By

WILLIAM LYON PHELPS

First published in 1927

British Library Cataloguing-in-Publication Data
A catalogue record for this book is available
from the British Library

CONTENTS

WILLIAM LYON PHELPS 5

HAPPINESS 7

WILLIAM LYON PHELPS

William Lyon Phelps was born on 2nd January 1865, in New Haven, Conneticut, United States.

Phelps earned a B.A. in 1887, writing his thesis on the Idealism of George Berkeley. He then gained an M.A. in 1891 from Yale and his PhD from Harvard in the same year.

During his time a Yale, he offered a course in modern novels which brought the university considerable attention both nationally and internationally. This was quite controversial at the time and Phelps was pressured to give up the course, but eventually, due to popular demand, reinstated it outside the official curriculum.

In 1892, Phelps married Annabel Hubbard, sister of childhood friend Frank Hubbard, and the couple moved to the family estate overlooking Lake Huron. Phelps christened it "The House of the Seven Gables", after the Nathanial Hawthorne story of the same name.

He became a very popular figure at Yale but also as an inspirational orator. He went on lecture tours that drew large audiences, speaking on the virtues of modern literature. He also preached regularly at the Huron City Methodist Episcopal Church and attracted such large crowds that the church was remodelled twice in five years to accommodate them.

Phelps published many essays on modern and European literature, including titles such as *Essays on Modern Novelists* (1910), *Some Makers of American Literature* (1923), and *As I Like it* (1923).

After his retirement from Yale in 1933, after 41 years of service, Phelps continued his public speaking, preaching, and writing a newspaper column. He also sat on book selection committees and acted as a judge for the Pulitzer Prize for literature.

His wife, Annabel, died from a stroke in 1939 and Phelps died four years later, in 1943.

HAPPINESS

NO MATTER WHAT may be one's nationality, sex, age, philosophy, or religion, everyone wishes either to become or to remain happy. Hence definitions of happiness are interesting. One of the best was given in my Senior year at college by President Timothy Dwight: "The happiest person is the person who thinks the most interesting thoughts."

This definition places happiness where it belongs-within and not without. The principle of happiness should be like the principle of virtue; it should not be dependent on things, but be a part of personality. Suppose you went to a member of a State Legislature, and offered him five hundred dollars to vote for a certain bill. Suppose he kicked you out of his office. Does that prove he is virtuous? No; it proves you can't buy him for five hundred. Suppose you went to the same man a month later and offered him a million dollars-that is, instead of making him a present, you make him and his family independent for life, for the best thing about having money is that if you have it, you don't have to think about it. Suppose, after listening to this offer, he should hesitate. That would mean he was already damned.

He is not only not virtuous, he knows nothing about virtue. Why? Because his virtue is dependent not on any interior standard, but on the size of the temptation. If the temptation is slight, he can resist; if alluring his soul is in danger. Such virtue is like being brave when there is no danger, generous when you have nothing to give, cheerful when all is well, polite when you are courteously treated.

Fortunately there are in every State Legislature some men who have no price, who are never for sale, who look upon all bribes with equal scorn-and these are the virtuous men. After the same order, there are boys who are just as safe in Paris as in Binghamton; just as safe at three o'clock in the morning as at three o'clock in the afternoon; just as safe with evil companions as with good companions. Why? Because these boys do not allow place, time, and people to determine their conduct, they attend to that matter themselves. Their standards are within.

So far as it is possible-it is not always possible-happiness should be like virtue. It should be kept or lost, not by exterior circumstances, but by an inner standard of life. Yet some readers of this page will lose their happiness before next Sunday, though I hope they recover it. But why lose it, even for a season? There are people who carry their happiness as a foolish woman carries a purse of money in her hand while walking on a crowded thoroughfare. The first man who is quick with his fingers, nimble with his feet, and untrammelled by conscience, can and will take the purse away, and disappear with it. He will have separated the woman and her money. Now if one's happiness is like that, an exterior thing, dependent on an enemy's volition, on a chance disaster, on an ill wind, on any one of a thousand accidents to which we are all exposed-then happiness can be lost.

All of us have enemies. I regard myself as on the whole an amiable person, and yet there are a considerable number of people, who, when they hear of my death, will feel relieved. I care as little about that fact now as I shall then. I do not intend to let other people, especially those who do not like me anyhow, determine whether I shall have peace of mind or not. If some one reports to you a malicious word that someone else has said of you, and in consequence of that, you become unhappy, you have allowed another person to hold the key of your heart, to settle whether you shall be happy or not. I insist that you ought to determine that question for yourself. Instead of being angry or distressed when people hate you, suppose you regard it as amusing; for if you are honestly trying to do your best, and incur hatred for your pains, there is about such a situation something funny. If you can appreciate the humour of it, you are free.

It is impossible for anyone to feel every moment exuberantly happy; to feel, on rising from bed every morning, like a young dog released from a chain. If you felt that way chronically, you would become an intolerable nuisance; you would get on everybody's nerves. But I am certain that with the correct philosophy, it is possible to have within one's personality sources of happiness that cannot permanently be destroyed. You will have days and nights of anguish, caused by ill-health, or worry, or losses, or the death of friends; but you will not remain in the Slough of Despond; you will rise above depression and disaster, because you will have within your mind the invincible happiness that comes from thinking interesting thoughts.

If the happiest person is the person who thinks the most interesting thoughts, then the mind is more important than either of those tremendous blessings, wealth and health. I never indulge in slighting remarks about money, because if I did, I should be a hypocrite. Money is a blessing; I should be glad to distribute a large sum to every one of my readers, of course reserving the usual commission. But money is not the chief factor in happiness. If it were, then everyone who had money would be happy and everyone without it would be unhappy; but there are so many wealthy people who are unhappy and so many poor people who are cheerful, that money, however important or desirable, is not the determining cause. It would be folly to speak slightingly of health. No one realises what a blessing health is until one has lost it; then one has to devote time and energy and money to recovering it. Anyone who is careless of his health is a traitor; because one's usefulness, one's capacity to do good in the world, is usually seriously lessened by poor health. Yet even health is not the sine qua non. People without it think they would be perfectly happy if they were well. A man with a toothache imagines that everyone in the world without a toothache is happy-but it is not so. There are healthy people who are not happy; and there are invalids whose faces, eyes, and conversation reveal an inner source of happiness that enables them to triumph over bodily ills. They have overcome the world, the flesh, and the devil.

I should be sorry to lose what money I have, but unfortunate as it might be, such a loss would not permanently destroy my happiness. I should be sorry to be run over by an automobile, and lose my right leg; but such a loss would not permanently destroy my happiness. Why not? Because my happiness is centred neither in my purse nor in my leg; but in my mind, my personality. The Irish dramatist, St. John Ervine, lost a leg in the war. I asked him which he would prefer, to have two sound and healthy legs again, and not be able to write novels and plays, or to be as he is now, with only one leg, but an accomplished man of letters? He did not hesitate. He said there was no comparison possible; he would far rather be a one-legged writer, than a two-legged something else. "And yet," he murmured thoughtfully, "I do miss that leg."

There is another important consideration. If the happiest person is the person who thinks the most interesting thoughts, then we grow happier as we grow older.

Of course I know that such a statement runs counter to the generally expressed opinion. The majority of novels and poems and the common gossip of society assume that youth is the golden time of life.

Yet ah! that Spring should vanish with the rose!
That youth's sweet-scented manuscript should close!
The nightingale that in the branches sang
flh, whence and whither flown again, who knows?

When I was an undergraduate, a distinguished man addressed us, and he said emphatically, "Young gentlemen, make the most of these four years; for they are the happiest years you will ever know." The remark was given to us with that impressiveness that so often accompanies a falsehood. For it was a falsehood.. My classmates and I have been out of college forty years; most of us are happier now than then.

I read many French novels, and I often see a woman of forty-five described as a "woman for whom life was over." Over at forty-five? and why? Because strange men do not stare at her. Doubtless it is sweet to be admired, doubtless flirtation is one of the normal pleasures of youth, doubtless it is agreeable to be regarded as a pretty animal; but is that all there is in life for a woman? One cannot penetrate below the surface of such a statement without finding an insult to personality.

No one should make a statement like "youth is the happiest time of life" without being prepared to accept its intellectual consequences. If it were really true that youth is the happiest time of life, nothing would be a more tragic spectacle than college boys and young maidens; for they would in their present state have attained the pinnacle, the climax of existence; before them lie fifty years of diminuendo, of decay, of accumulating loss, of descent into ever darkening days.

Some middle-aged silly women become romantically sad as they talk about what they are pleased to call their lost youth; I maintain that it is as absurd for a woman of fifty to mourn because she is no longer twenty as it would be for a woman of twenty to sob because she is no longer three. And indeed there are some idiots who declare that childhood is the happiest time of life. "Ah, that I were a child again!" Don't worry; you soon will be.

The belief that youth is the happiest time of life is founded on a fallacy-on a false definition of happiness. Many people think that to be free from physical pain and mental worry is perfection; knowing that as we grow older our physical pains and mental worries are apt to increase, they assume that youth is the happiest time of life. We are, of course, all animals; but we ought not to be merely animal. I suppose that in the case of animals, youth is the happiest time of life; a puppy is happier than an old rheumatic hound; a young jackass braying in the pasture is presumably happier than an old donkey laboriously drawing a cart; but these are merely animals, and lack man's greatest gift the possibility of development.

Those who say that childhood is the happiest time are unconsciously postulating the animal definition; a child is happiest because he is healthy and has no worries; when he is cold, somebody covers him; when he is hungry, somebody feeds him; when he is sleepy, somebody puts him to bed. Yes, but when he is not sleepy somebody puts him to bed. There is the shadow on the sunny years; there is the fly in the ointment. Personally I had rather have a few worries and aches, and go to bed when I choose. A child is as dependent as a slave. If you would rather be a healthy, welled slave than an independent man, you will prefer childhood to maturity. A child is at the mercy of adults both physically and mentally. They are stronger than he and can force him to do what they wish; they are cleverer than he, and can invariably outwit him. Let me give an illustration of both.

When I was six years old, I was playing ball with a contemporary. It was my ball, my property; that is to say, father had given it to me. Well, I made a muff, the ball rolled into the street, and a bigger boy grabbed it. "Here," I shouted, "give me that back. That's my ball."

"'Tain't yours now," said he,

with a disagreeable grin, "I've got it"

"No, but it don't belong to you, it's mine!"

"It ain't yours any longer," he rejoined, and he was correct. It wasn't. He has got it still. I never saw it again. All I could do was to sit down and cry. Do I want to be a child again?

At about the same age, I was fortunate enough to own a silver three cent piece. And in those days, one could really buy something for three cents. Not wishing to spend so large a sum at once, I decided to have it changed. I walked into a large grocery store, and asked the clerk to change my three cent piece. He looked at my insignificant figure and said curtly, "We haven't any change in the store," I withdrew and stood on the sidewalk. A fat Irishman came along and glancing at me, inquired what was the matter.

"The matter, Sir, is that I have a three cent piece and can't get it changed."

"Why don't you go into the store ?"

"They have no change in the store, Sir."

"How do you know that?" "They told me so, Sir."

"Sonny, you come along with me."

I put my tiny hand into the enormous paw of that Irishman, and we walked together into the store, and as luck would have it, we confronted exactly the same clerk who had informed me that there was no change. The Irishman said sharply, "This boy wants his three cent piece changed."

To my absolute amazement, the clerk said civilly, "Why, certainly," opened a drawer, and gave me three coppers. It was one of the first great surprises of my life. Upon reflection, I perceived that if you had no influence, there was no change; the fact was variable, depending simply upon the individual's power to command influence. Today I have both change and influence, and do not care to be a child again.

Happiness is not altogether a matter of luck. It is dependent on certain conditions. One should prepare for happiness as an athlete prepares for a contest. Leave out the things that injure, cultivate the things that strengthen, and good results follow. It is important to grow old successfully, for everyone must either grow old or die; and although the pessimists tell us that life is not worth living, I observe that most individuals hang on as long as they can. It is sad to see so many men and women afraid of growing old. They are in bondage to fear. Many of them, when they find the first grey hair, are alarmed. Now one really ought not to be alarmed when one's hair turns grey; if it turned green or blue, then one ought to see a doctor. But when it turns grey, that simply means there is so much grey matter in the skull there is no longer room for it; it comes out and discolours the hair. Don't be ashamed of your grey hair; wear it proudly, like a flag. You are fortunate, in a world of so many vicissitudes, to have lived long enough to earn it.

There are some foolish people who say, "Well, I mean to grow old gracefully." It is impossible; it can't be done. Let us admit it, because it is true; old people are not graceful. Grace belongs to youth and is its chief charm. The poet Browning hints that youth has beauty and grace because youth would be intolerable without it. Young people are decorative; that is why we like them. They are slender, agile, fair and graceful, because nobody could stand them if they were otherwise. It would be horrible if boys and girls, knowing as little as they do, were also bald, grey-headed, fat, wrinkled, and double-chinned; then they would be unendurable. But Nature has so arranged matters that young people are physically attractive until they acquire some brains and sense, and are able to live by their wits; then they lose these superficial advantages. As responsibility grows, beauty and grace depart. The child sits on your knee, and reaches for your watch. You smile, and say, "Nice baby, can't have de watch!" But when he is thirty and reaches for your watch, you put him in jail. More is expected of us, more is demanded of us, as we grow older; nothing is more tragic therefore than a woman of mature years with the mind of a child. There is in civilised society no place for her.

But even if it were possible to grow old gracefully, it would be at best a form of resignation, a

surrender; and a soldier of life should not take it lying down. Instead of growing old gracefully, suppose we grow old eagerly, grow old triumphantly. Is this possible? With the right mind and character, with the right attitude, with the right preparation, it is not only possible, it is probable. Joseph Ii. Choate was no deluded enthusiast; he was a hard-headed man of the world. When he was past seventy, in a public address in New York he maintained that the happiest time of life was between seventy and eighty years of age; "and I advise you all to hurry up and get there as soon as you can."

Let us examine another fallacy. It is said that as we grow older, we lose our illusions. Of course we do. I do not believe I have a single illusion left; if I have, I would gladly lose it today. For what

14

happens when you lose an illusion?

Every time you lose an illusion, you gain a new idea. Ideas are more interesting, hence pleasuregiving, than illusions. The world as it is, men and women as they are, are more worth knowing than fancy pictures created by ignorance and inexperience. We are told that youth is happy because youth looks on the world through rosecoloured spectacles. But I have no desire to look at the world through rose-coloured spectacles, and I can prove that you haven't. That repository of wisdom and experience, Robert Browning, at the age of seventy-seven, wrote

Friend, did you need an optic glass,

Which were your choice? If lens to drape

In ruby, emerald, chrysopras, Each object-or reveal its shape Clear outlined, past escape,

The naked very thing?-so clear That, when you had the chance to gaze,

You found its inmost self appear Through outer seeming-truth ablaze,

Not falsehood's fancy-haze?

This can very easily be determined by our old friend in political economy, the law of supply and demand. Demand fixes the price; a thing in great demand is worth more than something for which the demand is feeble. Suppose you were going to Europe this summer, and stopped in at the optician's to buy a pair of powerful binoculars. Suppose he should suggest that instead of getting that, you took a kaleidoscope, where instead of looking at distant objects, you saw pretty rosettes, bright combinations of coloured glass. "Do you think I am a child, to be amused with rose-coloured toys?" "Ah, but distance lends enchantment to the view; when you see a ship five miles away, she is as beautiful as a swan. But if you look at her with binoculars, you see shreds and patches, washing hanging on the deck-lines, and other realities. Surely you don't want the truth."

Surely you do. And the proof is that anyone can buy rose - coloured glasses cheaply, but every time you increase the power of the lens, that is every time you bring reality nearer, the price goes up enormously. If then we are willing to pay cash to substitute truth for illusion, let us be done with saying that youth is happy because of illusion. As we grow older, our eyes become achromatic; rose - colours fall away, and we see life more nearly as it is, and find it more interesting.

It is also often said that as we grow older, we lose our enthusiasms. This need not be true; it is never true with right-minded individuals. There is a fallacy lurking in such a statement. The fallacy is this; we confound the loss of the object that aroused our enthusiasm with the loss of enthusiasm, a very different thing. Things that excite children often fail to arouse mature men and women-which is not a sign that maturity has lost sensitiveness to excitement; it may have lost interest in childish things. When I was a child, the happiest day in the year was the Fourth of July. It was not illusory happiness; it was real; it was authentic bliss. Its cause? On the Fourth of July my mother allowed me to rise at midnight, go out on the street and yell till daybreak. Think of it, I, who usually was forced to retire at eight, was out on a city street at three in the morning, shrieking and yelling! It was delirious joy. Now suppose you should tell me that tomorrow I may rise at midnight and yell till daybreak. I decline.

Does that mean I have lost my happiness, or my enthusiasm? No; it means that I don't care to rise at midnight. During the daytime of the glorious Fourth, I used to shoot off firecrackers hour after hour, with undiminished zeal. Every now and then, I would see a very old man, about thirty-two, come along, and I would offer him an opportunity to share my delight. He always declined. "Poor fellow!" I reflected, "Life is over for him. He has lost his happiness." It never occurred to me that people over thirty had any fun. I supposed they had to go through the routine of life, but had no pleasure in it.

The fact that a girl of three is enchanted by the gift of a doll, and the same girl at seventeen insulted by it, does not mean that the girl at seventeen has lost either her happiness or her enthusiasm; but that the enthusiasm, formerly aroused by dolls, is now stimulated by something else.

If the happiest person is the person who thinks the most interesting thoughts, we are bound to grow happier as we advance in years, because our minds have more and more interesting thoughts. A well-ordered life is like climbing a tower; the view half way up is better than the view from the base, and it steadily becomes finer as the horizon expands. Herein lies the real value of education. Advanced education may or may not make men and women more efficient; but it enriches personality, increases the wealth of the mind, and hence brings happiness. It is the finest insurance against old age, against the growth of physical disability, of the lack and loss of animal delights. No matter how many there may be in our family, no matter how many friends we may have, we are in a certain sense forced to lead a lonely life, because we have all the days of our existence to live with ourselves. How essential it is then, to acquire some intellectual or artistic tastes, in order to furnish the mind, to be able to live inside a mind with attractive and interesting pictures on the walls! It is better to be an interesting personality than to be an efficient machine. Many go to destruction by the alcoholic route because they cannot endure themselves; the moment they are left alone with their empty minds, they seek for stimulant, for something to make them forget the waste places. Others rush off to the motion-pictures, run anywhere, always seeking something to make them forget themselves.

Higher education, the cultivation of the mind, is more important for women than for men; because women are more often left alone. A large part of masculine activity is merely physical; men run around like dogs. But a woman, even in these emancipated days, is forced to be alone more than man. Now take the instance of a girl who has been brought up happily in a large family, with plenty of neighbours and friends, whose bright days pass in happy activities and recreations; she is married to a suburbanite in New Jersey. Every morning he takes the 7.37 train to New York, and

does not return till the 6.48 in the evening. The young wife, rudely transplanted from a cheerful home, is placed in an empty house, in a town where she knows no one, and is alone all day. God help her if she has no mental interests, no ideas, no interesting thoughts

I have no desire to underestimate the worth of physical comfort, or the charm of youth; but if happiness truly consisted in physical ease and freedom from care, then the happiest individual would not be either a man or a woman. It would be, I think, an American cow. American cows and American dogs are ladies and gentlemen

of leisure; in Europe they hitch them up and make them draw loads. Take therefore an average day in the life of an American cow, and we shall see that it is not far from the commonly accepted ideal of human happiness. The cow rises in the morning and with one flick of her tail, her toilet is completed for the whole day. This is a distinct advantage over humanity. It takes the average woman (and it ought to) about threequarters of an hour every single day to arrange her appearance. When Harriet Martineau was a child, she was appalled by the prospect of having to brush her teeth every day of her life. She lived to be ninety. The cow does not have to brush her teeth; the cow does not have to bob her hair; the cow does not have to select appropriate and expensive garments; or carry a compact; one flick, and she is ready. And when she is ready, breakfast is ready. She does not have to light the kitchen fire herself, or to mourn because the cook has left without notice. The grass is her cereal breakfast and the dew thereupon is the cream. After eating for an hour or so, she gazes meditatively into the middle distance querying first, whether that grass yonder is lusher and greener than this, and second, if it be so, whether peradventure it is worth the trouble to walk there and take it.

Such an idea as that will occupy the mind of a cow for three hours. After grazing, without haste and without rest, she reaches by noon the edge of a stream. "Lo, here is water; what hinders me from descending and slaking my thirst?" She descends about waist deep into the cooling stream; and after external and internal refreshment, she walks with dignity to the shade of a spreading tree, and sits down calmly in the shadow. There and then she begins to chew the cud. Her upper jaw remains stationary, while the lower revolves in a kind of solemn rapture; there is on her placid features no pale cast of thought; the cow chewing the cud has very much the expression of a healthy American girl chewing gum. I never see one without thinking of the other. The eyes of a cow are so beautiful that Homer gave them to the Queen of Heaven, because he could not think of any other eyes so large, so lustrous, so liquid, and so untroubled. Cows are never perturbed by introspection or by worry. There are no agnostic cows; no Fundamentalist or Modernist cows; cows do not worry about the income tax or the league of nations; a cow does not lie awake at night wondering if her son is going to the devil in some distant city. Cows have none of the thoughts that inflict upon humanity distress and torture. I have observed many cows, and there is in their beautiful eyes no perplexity; their serene faces betray no apprehension or alarm; they are never even bored. They have found some happy via media by which they escape from Schopenhauer's dilemma, who insisted that man had only the vain choice between the suffering of unsatisfied desire and the languor of ennui.

Well, since the daily life of an American cow is ,exactly the existence held up to us as ideal - physical comfort with no pains and no worries, who wouldn't be a cow? Very few human beings would be willing to change into cows, which must mean only one thing. Life, with all its sorrows, cares, perplexities, and heartbreaks, is more interesting than bovine placidity, hence more desirable. The more interesting it is, the happier it is. And the happiest person is the person who thinks the most interesting thoughts.